more than the score...

ERIK SATIE

Gnossienne No. 3

for piano solo

Presented by Joanna MacGregor

Contents

Joanna MacGregor talks about
Satie's *Gnossienne* No. 3 2

Gnossienne No. 3 4

About the composer 6

About the music 6

This publication draws on material released by
Edition Peters in the *Piano Masterworks* collection on
Tido Music, a revolutionary web resource and iPad app.

PETERS EDITION LTD

A member of the EDITION PETERS GROUP
LEIPZIG · LONDON · NEW YORK

Published by Peters Edition Ltd, London
2–6 Baches Street   London N1 6DN
www.editionpeters.com
This edition © 2017 by Peters Edition Ltd, London

Joanna MacGregor

talks about

Satie's *Gnossienne* No. 3

Satie was very keen on inventing his own titles and making up words. 'Gnossienne' is a made-up word. No one really knows what it means, but it does derive from 'Knossos', and it reminds us of the island of Crete where people had just discovered this ancient city. It reminds us that's where the minotaur and the labyrinth come from. If you keep all these things in mind – ancient Greece, a labyrinth, a mystery that no one can solve – this is a pretty good zone for your head to be in when you're playing Satie.

Satie uses the Lydian mode; almost like white-note music. It's not the same scale or same tonality that Bach would have written in; it's more folky, almost.

Gnossienne No. 3 presents a paradox because, in many ways, it's very free. It looks free because there are no barlines or time signatures, and there's very little in the way of dynamics. However, there is a left-hand pattern that's absolutely constant and consistent.

A very nice way of practising this is with four hands. You, or somebody else, could play the left-hand part in two hands, and somebody else could play the right hand. The reason why I suggest you practise this in two hands is that you'll begin to get a sense of the calm that you need just to move from harmony to harmony. It's the same rhythmic pattern all the way through, but it needs to sound rather neutral. You don't want ever to sound dramatic or agitated with it; you've got to have a kind of neutrality in the way you play.

Dynamics and pedalling

The main theme at the beginning of this *Gnossienne* repeats over and over again. It is slightly mysterious and sounds slightly Eastern-European. Because this figure repeats so often, I think it's perfectly all right for you to choose different dynamics as you repeat.

Watch out for the pedalling, because you have long notes that have to last through the harmony, so you need to keep that pedal down. Change the pedal with each of the low notes. This is quite important because this will affect how you play your melody. It's very important that your pedalling is very accurate. You don't want to blur the harmonies. Don't try and make sense of the harmony. The point about Satie is that he writes in blocks. He's not like Bach who journeys from key to key. He's a different kind of composer.

> *The point about Satie is that he writes in blocks*

Your right hand, in general, needs to lift it off from the keyboard. The reason for that is that the pedal unfortunately makes everything last, because you've got to pedal the left hand through, the harmonies through. But if you just remember to lift your right hand off the keyboard, at least you follow the shape of the right hand more. There are some breaths in the right hand, there's a sense in which there are rests where you're not playing, and so do try and lift the hand as you play, don't just let it sit on the keyboard.

Rubato

You have the chance to play with a bit of rubato in this music because, although you have this almost rocking, very consistent left hand, your right hand can weave a bit, and it's a little bit like playing a Chopin Nocturne. You want to find a way where there's some consistency, but within that, there's a lot of suppleness, and your hand literally has to be supple. Again, keep it feeling very loose, very relaxed. You want to have a right hand that just moves around like a dancer. Actually, Satie helps by putting in the old hairpin dynamics.

Satie does something which I call 'going for a walk'. He takes the music for a walk, really, because in some ways, he's set this melodic phrase, and we've got the consistency of the left hand, and then suddenly he decides, 'Of course that's not enough', and he takes you somewhere, but it's a bit directionless, it's slightly meandering, but it's a nice thing to play.

Harmonic language

Satie constantly breaks rules harmonically, and he does it deliberately. He always liked to think that he was self-taught and self-trained, and he hadn't been a student, he hadn't studied music anywhere, and so you want to enjoy these sudden shifts in harmony, because they're deliberately sort of un-academic. It's like someone's sitting at the piano and making it up a bit, and just enjoying lots of chords and harmonies: you must be like that, too. Don't try and make sense of these changes.

The other thing about the piece is it just stops: he doesn't prepare you for it or indicate you can slow down, or any of those things, so it's quite fun deciding whether you're going to stop it quite shockingly. It's quite a beautiful piece of music, so you want to try and do a bit of that, but maybe just round off the sound a little bit. Round the sound off with your pedalling. It's a sort of version of stopping, but not in such a violent way.

Tempo

Satie could have given us a metronome mark, but he doesn't, of course – that's not his style. He just says it's *lent*, it's slow. There are lots of different ways of interpreting that. I think my rule with Satie, like with Bach, is that it should never be boring, so if you pick a slow tempo and it starts to sound dull, or it starts to get so slow we're all falling asleep, it's clearly too slow. You need to find an atmosphere that feels ancient, full of memory, full of longing, full of melancholy.

Erik Satie, oil portrait by Suzanne Valadon, 1893

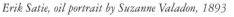

The thing to remember about Erik Satie is that he is a jester; he's someone who likes playing pranks

It doesn't have to go that slowly; you're looking for an atmosphere, really. I think the tough thing is finding a speed that enables you to manage your left hand without too much bumping and crashing, because it's very easy to make the leap and then to bump on to the chord. You need to be patient, you'll find, because you need to practise those jumps.

Humour

The thing to remember about Erik Satie is that he is a jester; he's someone who likes playing pranks, and he's got a sense of humour, which is always difficult in classical music, because we like to think that all classical music's very serious and profound. Satie is funny: he's quite sharp in his looking at society and making appraisals. Often in his music, he puts these rather mysterious French phrases, which are incredibly hard to decipher and to know what they mean or what the point of them is, or if they're trying to give you indications. I think he often puts something in because he's an absurdist and a surrealist.

There are two bits of French advice in this piece that I find really helpful, and I think they are quite meaningful – although I'm not quite sure how they make me want to play. In the second half of the piece, he writes, 'Très perdu' (very lost): think of this as music that's walking around a bit, it's gone for a walk, your right hand is walking up and down the keyboard; the second time you're playing it you need to sound as though you're lost, and he actually says this again in another *Gnossienne*. He obviously likes this as a direction. I would interpret it as having less of a sound, having a more transparent sound, so it's not so tonal.

The other thing he says in the second half of the piece is, 'Ouvrez la tête' (open your head), which I think is a great piece of advice. Who knows what you might find there? He writes it over the F minor section, which is quite a surprising key change. Again, you can give your playing a surprising quality of sound: 'I opened my head, and I can't believe what I saw in there!'

Joanna MacGregor is one of the world's most innovative musicians. Head of Piano at the Royal Academy of Music, London, and Professor at the University of London, she is also Artistic Director of Dartington International Summer School & Festival

Gnossienne No. 3

from *Trois Gnossiennes*

Erik Satie (1866–1925)

Lent

Conseillez-vous soigneusement

Munissez-vous de clairvoyance

Seul, pendant un instant

De manière à obtenir un creux

Edition Peters 73159

Très perdu

Portez cela plus loin

Ouvrez la tête

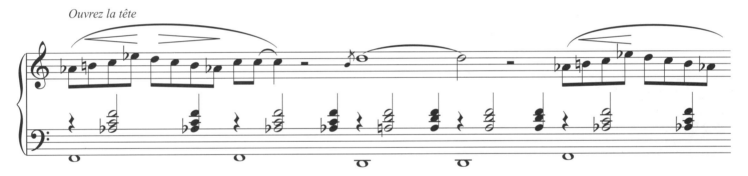

Enfouissez le son

About Erik Satie...

Erik Satie, c. 1919

Satie was born in Normandy in 1866. His career began as a café pianist and conductor in the Montmartre cabarets. Here, he developed an acute awareness of artistic currents that was to underpin his own creative output, even if he was to deliberately set himself apart from musical fashion and, as a result, foreshadow most of the major trends of the twentieth century. His response to Debussy's advice that he 'develop his sense of form' was to compose a work entitled *Three pieces in the form of a pear*.

Nevertheless, Satie's quest to be taken seriously as a composer was real and earnest. In 1905 he enrolled at the Schola Cantorum to study orchestration, fugue and counterpoint. In the immediate pre-war period, Satie – now hailed by Debussy as 'the precursor' – earned publications, concerts and the acclaim of the younger generation. By early 1925, however, the ill-effects of a lifetime spent in bars and cabarets could no longer be ignored and he died on 1 July.

Emily Kilpatrick

Trois Gnossiennes...

Grand Staircase of Knossos, the palace of King Minos in Crete, Greece. Photo: Stefan Bellini

Erik Satie's *Trois Gnossiennes* were composed in the early 1890s. The title is a word of Satie's invention: like the *Gymnopédies*, it evokes ancient Greece gesturing both to Knossos (a famous Bronze Age archaeological site on Crete) and to Gnosticism (which entails a quest for spiritual wisdom and enlightenment). Languid dances, with ostinato accompaniments, slow-moving – almost static – harmonies and sinuous melodies, the *Trois Gnossiennes* are musical cousins of the *Gymnopédies*, though they employ more exotic modal colours suggesting a response to the Javanese gamelan and Romanian folk musics that impressed Satie at the Paris Exposition.

The pieces – in which Satie dispenses with barlines and time signatures – date from the period in which Satie was involved both with the (specious) Rosicrucian order, and working as a cabaret pianist and conductor in the Montmartre clubs. This is reflected in their enigmatic and peculiar performance instructions and likely use as accompaniment to shadow theatre performances in such clubs. The *Gnossiennes* were not published until 1913, resulting from the world's belated 'discovery' of Satie in 1911 and his works now being regarded as progressive rather than mystic.

Emily Kilpatrick

TIDO

Transform your piano playing

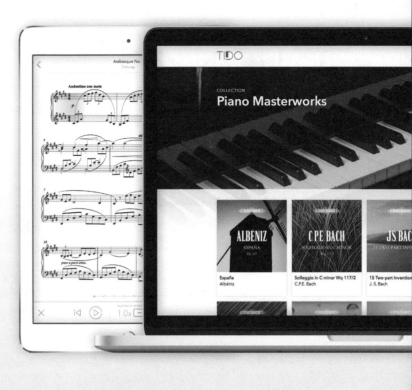

Tido Music is a revolutionary web resource for the discovery, study and performance of piano music.

Enjoy unlimited access to a growing library of sheet music online, brought to life with recordings, video performances and more.

Whether you're a student, a teacher or an advanced pianist, Tido will guide and inspire you.

Piano Masterworks, the first collection to appear on the platform, launched with content from Edition Peters.

Enhance your experience with Tido Music for iPad

- The app listens to you play and turns pages automatically!

- Leading pianists share insight on technique and interpretation in video masterclasses

EDITION PETERS
LEIPZIG · LONDON · NEW YORK

TIDO

TIDO

Piano Masterworks

The rapidly expanding *Piano Masterworks* collection includes the following titles from Edition Peters:

Albéniz, I.	España Op. 165
Bach, J. S.	15 Two-part Inventions; French Suite No. 5; Goldberg Variations; The Well-tempered Clavier, Book 1; The Well-tempered Clavier, Book 2; 15 Three-part Inventions (Sinfonias); Partita No. 4 in D major; Toccata in D minor; Italian Concerto
Bach, C. P. E.	Solfeggio H220
Beethoven, L. van	Bagatelles; Für Elise; Sonata 'Pathétique' in C minor; Sonata in G major Op. 49 No. 2; 'Moonlight' Sonata in C sharp minor; Sonata in F minor Op. 2 No. 1; 'The Tempest' Sonata in D minor; 6 Variations in F major
Brahms, J.	4 Piano Pieces Op. 119; 6 Piano Pieces Op. 118; 3 Intermezzi Op. 117
Cage, J.	A Room; Dream; In a Landscape; Opening Dance for Sue Laub; Suite for Toy Piano; Three Easy Pieces
Chopin, F.	Waltz in C sharp minor Op. 64 No. 2; 24 Préludes Op. 28
Clementi, M.	Sonatinas Op. 36
Debussy, C.	Deux Arabesques; Children's Corner; La Cathédrale Engloutie; Suite Bergamasque
Fauré, G.	Pavane Op. 50; Pièces Brèves Op. 84
Field, J.	Nocturnes
Grieg, E.	Holberg Suite Op. 40; Lyric Pieces Book 1; Lyric Pieces Book 2
Handel, G. F.	Suite No. 5 in E Major 'The Harmonious Blacksmith'
Haydn, J.	Sonata in D major Hob. XVI:37
Janáček, L.	On an Overgrown Path
Liszt, F.	Consolations; Liebesträume; 2 Pieces from Weihnachtsbaum
Mendelssohn, F.	Songs Without Words Book 1; Songs Without Words Book 6
Mozart, W. A.	Adagio for Glass Harmonica; Adagio in B minor; Fantasy in D minor; Sonata in C major; Sonata in A minor
Musorgsky, M.	Pictures from an Exhibition
Ravel, M.	À la Manière de Chabrier; Pavane pour une Infante défunte
Satie, E.	3 Gnossiennes; 3 Gymnopédies
Schubert, F.	Impromptu in E flat major; Impromptu in G flat major; 6 Moments Musicaux
Scriabin, A.	Etude in C sharp minor; Prelude in C sharp minor (for Left Hand)
Scarlatti, D.	Sonata in E major K162
Schumann, R.	Album for the Young; Scenes from Childhood; Waldszenen
Tchaikovsky, P. I.	The Seasons; Album for the Young